AUTO MECHANIC

Aileen Weintraub

HIGH
interest
books

Children's Press®
A Division of Scholastic Inc.
New York / Toronto / London / Auckland / Sydney
Mexico City / New Delhi / Hong Kong
Danbury, Connecticut

Book Design: Christopher Logan and Daniel Hosek
Layout and Production: Mindy Liu
Photo Credits: Cover, p. 22 © Royalty-Free/Corbis; p. 4 © James A. Sugar/Corbis; p. 7 © Charles Gupton/Corbis; pp. 8, 12 © Bettmann/Corbis; p. 11 © Hulton/Archive/Getty Images; p. 15 © Ray Juno/Corbis; p. 16 © Shepard Sherbell/Corbis Saba; p. 19 © Hekimian Julien/Corbis Sygma; pp. 21, 25, 36, 39, 40–41 © AP/Wide World Photos; p. 26 © George D. Lepp/Corbis; p. 29 © Reuters NewMedia Inc./Corbis; pp. 31, 34 © William Taufic/Corbis

Library of Congress Cataloging-in-Publication Data

Weintraub, Aileen, 1973–
    Auto mechanic / Aileen Weintraub.
    p. cm. — (Great jobs)
    Includes bibliographical references and index.
    Contents: Start your engines — Getting in gear — Under the hood — Popular mechanics.
    ISBN 0-516-24090-0 (lib. bdg.) — ISBN 0-516-25922-9 (pbk.)
    1. Automobiles—Maintenance and repair—Vocational guidance—Juvenile literature. 2. Automobile mechanics—Juvenile literature. [1. Automobiles—Maintenance and repair—Vocational guidance. 2. Vocational guidance.] I. Title. II. Series.

TL152.W394 2003
629.28'72'023—dc22

                                         2003015396

2 3 4 5 6 7 8 9 10 R 13 12 11 10 09 08 07 06 05

Contents

Introduction

The phone is ringing off the hook. Three customers are anxiously waiting for attention. There is so much noise in the garage, Dave can hardly hear himself think. He has a pile of papers on his desk to fill out and two more customers to call back. On top of all that, the parts Dave ordered five days ago still haven't arrived.

Dave washes his hands, which are covered with grease. He wonders how much longer before his lunch break begins. He looks at the clock above the sink. It's only 9:50 in the morning.

It's another day packed with demands and high pressure, but Dave wouldn't have it any other way. As a senior auto mechanic, Dave must juggle a dozen tasks at once. He must take the time to answer questions and talk patiently with each one of his customers.

Mechanics do more than fix a car's problems—they must also make the car owner feel certain that the problem won't happen again.

For some people, a car is one of their most prized possessions. It may be the most expensive thing a person owns. Everyone wants and needs their car to run safely. They may rely on it to take them to work and school. They also may depend on it for long vacations, as well as quick trips to the supermarket.

Many people worry about bringing their car to a mechanic. They may not know exactly what is wrong with it. They do know, however, that fixing the problem is going to cost them money. They also know that while the car is being fixed, they must make other arrangements for getting around.

Drivers depend on Dave to spot problems and fix their cars. It is the mechanic's job to play detective. Dave may ask customers if a car is making any unusual sounds. He will want to know about any funny smells in the car. Dave must accurately determine what exactly is causing the car not to perform well. He must try to fix each car as quickly as possible. It's up to Dave to get his customers back on the road.

Some car owners develop such a level of trust with their personal mechanic that they wouldn't think of taking their car to someone else for repairs.

CHAPTER ONE

Start Your Engines

The Early Years

The automobile was invented in the late nineteenth century. It dramatically changed how and where people could travel. Cars allowed people to go to places they could once only dream of.

In the United States, fascination with cars grew quickly. However, many important people were slow to accept the advantages of automobiles. Presidents Woodrow Wilson and Theodore Roosevelt thought very little about the first motorcars. They claimed to have no interest in this new form of transportation. Both leaders changed their minds, though. Roosevelt would soon become the first president to own and drive a car.

At first, President Theodore Roosevelt was no fan of the automobile. However, the vehicle's convenience eventually won Roosevelt over.

TAKING CARE OF BUSINESS

The first speeder was arrested in 1899. He was racing along a roadway at a mere 12 miles (19.3 kilometers) an hour! The officer who arrested him was riding a bicycle.

Fitting Drivers to a T

In the early twentieth century, companies that manufactured cars began popping up all over. Each one tried to convince Americans that their product was the best. Many of these companies failed.

One company that thrived, however, was started by Henry Ford. The Ford Motor Company was destined for greatness. Those who loaned Ford money to build his business argued that his cars should only be driven by the wealthy. Ford refused to listen. He said he wanted to "build a car...so low in price that no man will be unable to own one."

He set off to do just that. The Ford Model T, developed in 1908, was the first mass-produced car. Each Model T was built on an assembly line.

Henry Ford wanted his car to be owned by as many Americans as possible. This photo proves his success. He's standing between the first Model T and the ten millionth!

Fifty workers stood along a moving track. They added new parts to the car as it moved down the track. Slowly, the Model T took shape. It took twelve hours to build one. Eventually, Ford got the time down to ninety minutes.

Thanks to the Model T, people no longer had to be wealthy to own a car. Suddenly, driving was affordable for many Americans. The Model T's price started at $850. As its popularity grew, the cost went down to $250. The last Model T was made in 1927. By that time, it had proved its claim as the

car of choice in the United States. Over 15 million people owned one!

Early Problems

Early cars had their share of mechanical problems. However, they were quite different from the problems that today's cars face. For example, cloth curtains were used to protect early automobiles from rainstorms. Sometimes, though, car owners couldn't get these curtains to shut properly. If the curtains didn't close, it would be hard to keep a car's charcoal heater dry. Also, the lamp on the front of the car, called a carbide lamp, often flickered on and off without warning. This made it impossible to see at night.

Most car owners stored their automobiles indoors during the winter months. At the time, there was nothing to protect cars from harsh winters. Antifreeze, winter oils, and good heaters hadn't yet been invented.

In the early twentieth century, Henry Ford's assembly line built Model Ts at a rapid rate. Yet workers could barely keep up with customer demand.

The power that drives today's assembly lines relies on high-tech computerized machines as much as it does on men and women.

Getting Better All the Time

As years went by, cars were given more features. Between 1920 and 1940, windshield wipers and radios were added. Wider tires were developed to give cars a better grip on the road. Air-conditioning and wrap-around windshields were introduced soon after that.

With each decade, companies were making cars that gave their drivers a smoother and safer ride. Cars could be driven at higher speeds and handled better than ever before. Braking systems improved. It soon became common for families to own two or even three cars. Of course, this made auto mechanics more important than ever.

TAKING CARE OF BUSINESS

In 1907, John McLean set up the nation's first roadside service station. The station was located in Seattle, Washington. McLean's station included a hot water tank and a hose under a wooden canopy.

Being a mechanic has changed a lot since those days of the Model T. Today's mechanics have to keep up with ever-changing technology. Most modern cars have about fifteen computers. There weren't that many computers on the first spacecraft! Computers operate everything from a car's air conditioner to its engine.

To properly repair modern cars, today's mechanics must understand math and science. After all, electric failure is now one of the leading causes of car trouble. Mechanics must also be comfortable with new technology, such as computers that help diagnose a car's problems.

CHAPTER TWO

Getting in Gear

Technology has had a huge impact on the way cars run. Cars are also made up of more materials than they used to be. Everything from aluminum and steel to plastics goes into building a car. Mechanics must know how to work with all of these materials. They must be able to understand new technology, as well as complex technical manuals. Most employers only hire mechanics who have completed a training program.

High School Training

Anyone interested in being an auto mechanic can begin his or her training in high school. It's important to take as many math and science courses as possible. Some high schools offer programs where a

Aspiring mechanics must combine hands-on experience with the knowledge they learn from books and manuals.

Apprenticeships help younger mechanics pick up tricks of the trade from more experienced technicians.

student can "shadow" a mechanic. In these programs, students follow an experienced mechanic through an entire workday. They watch everything from typing out a repair order (RO) to ordering parts.

One high school program is geared especially to future mechanics. It's known as Automotive Youth Education Service (AYES). Students who complete AYES receive more than a high school diploma. They also receive certification as an auto technician.

Advanced Studies

Many trade schools and community colleges specialize in training future mechanics. These schools combine classroom time with hands-on learning. Their training programs can last anywhere from six months to two years.

The best programs prepare students for Automotive Service Excellence (ASE) certification. ASE certifications put students on the path to getting a job. The more skills in which a mechanic is certified, the more work he or she will likely get.

Other Options

Many companies that make and sell cars sponsor their own training programs. In these cases, students spend up to twelve weeks in a classroom. After completing the classwork, they spend twelve more weeks working for the company.

The best mechanics work well under pressure. That's why some training programs now include stress management classes. After all, many customers who bring their cars in for repair are anxious.

They may act out in anger or frustration. Mechanics who can be patient and friendly with their clients often earn a customer for life.

Finding a Job

Most auto mechanics work for repair shops. Some of these places of business are independently owned. Some are national chains, such as Pep Boys. Other mechanics work for car dealerships. Some may work for trucking companies. Still others may work at gas stations.

Beginning auto mechanics will often work as apprentices assisting more experienced mechanics. Apprentices remove damaged car parts and install new ones. They may also do small repairs, such as fixing dents. It can take four years to become a fully skilled mechanic. Those with vocational school training may arrive at this level of expertise faster.

As mechanics learn new skills, their pay goes up. Most mechanics earn between $20,000 and $35,000

These days, there is a shortage of auto mechanics in the United States. This fact has helped open the door for more women to make their mark in the repair garage.

at first. They may also get commissions. This means that the more work they complete, the more they get paid. All their training pays off by the time they become master mechanics. Master mechanics make up to $100,000 a year.

Many mechanics work on cars that don't need repairs. The cars may not even be having any problems at all. These cars have been taken in for maintenance. All automobiles need to be checked on a regular basis. By having this service performed,

drivers can be assured their vehicles are running properly. It's similar to when men and women visit the doctor's office for a yearly checkup and physical examination. There may be nothing wrong with the patient. However, a checkup provides a good way of discovering problems before they occur.

Expert Advice

Many mechanics choose to focus on one specific area of car maintenance. For example, some technicians

TAKING CARE OF BUSINESS

Some mechanics choose to join labor unions. Labor unions make contracts that help protect their members. For instance, the contracts may offer better job safety. Unions also help fight for fair pay and medical care.

may work only on a car's transmission. The transmission is the part of the car that sends power from the engine to the driveshaft. A car's transmission is made up of over three thousand parts. No wonder it takes an expert to work on it!

Tune-up mechanics are experts at adjusting a car's ignition timing and valves. They replace spark plugs and help the engine run better. A front-end mechanic works on aligning and balancing a car's wheels. Front-end mechanics also repair the part of the car responsible for steering. There are even some specialists who only work on a car's air conditioner.

Mechanics expect to get down and dirty in the course of a day's work. This technician is working beneath a car to fix it.

Sometimes a car that has just been in an accident will be brought into a repair shop. Wrecked or damaged cars are taken care of by auto body repair specialists. They straighten out the bends in a car's damaged body. They remove dents, as well. If there's a small pit in the vehicle's metal, they may smooth it out with a pick hammer. The name of this technique is metal finishing.

Tools of the Trade

Generally, a mechanic's workplace will provide the more expensive power tools. However, many auto mechanics must purchase their own hand tools. Mechanics often will spend thousands of dollars to buy these tools. They often buy their own hammers to knock out dents. Pliers, screwdrivers, and wrenches are also essential tools to own.

One large-scale tool a repair shop might provide is a metal-cutting gun. This tool is used to cut off panels on a car that are too damaged to repair. After removing a damaged panel, mechanics will weld on a replacement panel.

This Nashville, Tennessee, repair garage stays open until midnight. Keeping such late hours helps customers who can't leave their jobs to get their vehicles repaired.

What if the problem isn't under the car's hood, but under the entire body of the car? In that case, mechanics place a rack beneath the car. They then turn on a switch. Suddenly, a system of hydraulics lifts the car several feet off the ground. This helps mechanics see what's underneath. It also allows them easy access to an automobile's inner workings.

CHAPTER THREE

Under the Hood

Linda's Day

Linda arrives for work at 7:30 A.M. She is an auto mechanic at a large repair garage. She has worked at the garage for ten years.

Linda begins her day by checking her work orders. These can range from changing a flat tire to overhauling a car's electrical system. Linda looks over her stack of orders. Suddenly, she hears Greg, her apprentice, call out, "Good morning."

"Hope you got enough sleep last night," Linda says, sorting the thick stack of orders. "We've got a full slate of jobs today."

Outside the garage, customers drop off their cars for repair. They explain to the garage service manager what problems their vehicles are having.

Some mechanics have to repair vehicles on extremely tight timetables. This technician is working on a car at a California raceway.

Depending on how severe a car's problems are, it may take a whole team of mechanics to get the vehicle back on the road.

The service manager writes down notes based on these complaints.

Service managers match mechanics to each job. They know the expertise of each mechanic on staff. They also know which employees can't handle certain jobs. For instance, a service manager won't assign a transmission job to a mechanic who isn't ASE-certified in that area.

Later, That Same Day

At 11 A.M., the garage is filled with crashing sounds. Power tools buzz. Hammers bang into metal panels. It's noisy, but Linda doesn't mind. She enjoys spending her days with coworkers who share her love for automobiles.

Greg, her apprentice, has taken a few classes at a nearby community college. Now he's eager to get some hands-on experience. When she sees a work order for a light blue 1967 Ford Thunderbird, Linda decides to let Greg work on it. After all, changing a tire is only a small job—and Linda knows Greg has a passion for classic cars.

After Linda finishes supervising Greg's work on the Thunderbird, she talks to an upset customer. The customer's car isn't starting properly. The first thing Linda does is to try to start the car herself. When she turns the key in the ignition, the dashboard lights fail to come on. Next, she checks the car battery to see if it's charged. She does this using a voltmeter. This tool measures and displays the voltage of the battery. Finally, Linda checks the wires—and that's when she uncovers the problem. The wiring for the battery is corroded. It will have to be replaced.

Motor Medicine

Mechanics like Linda are often compared to doctors. People come into the shop and describe their car's symptoms. Mechanics listen, then use their diagnostic skills to test the cars. They test different parts of the car to see if they're working properly. Mechanics may drive the car to see how it runs. They use their senses of sight, hearing, and even smell to determine problems.

For some mechanics, this is the best part of the job. It gives them a chance to put their skills and training to work. They know it's up to them to uncover a car's problems, solve them, and get the car back on the road as quickly as possible.

Routine Inspections

Mechanics often work on cars before the trouble starts. These jobs are called routine inspections. During an inspection, mechanics check the engine. They make sure all the car's fluids are at the right levels. They make sure that the belts, hoses, plugs, and brake systems are in good working order.

This car is already in good working order. By putting it through a routine inspection, the mechanic hopes to keep the car problem free for many more miles.

During inspections, Linda repairs and replaces any part that looks worn out or damaged. This will keep the car from breaking down. Sometimes, these repairs come at a steep cost. However, taking these precautions now will save the customer more headaches—and more money—down the line.

For Linda, there is no such thing as a routine day. She may work on up to ten cars in a single shift. On other days, she spends every working hour on one car. An oil change may mean only a few minutes of work. If Linda is fixing a transmission, she may devote several days to the job.

By 4 P.M., Linda is set to work on her last job of the day. She's fixing a broken air conditioner. She's hoping it will just have a low level of coolant. Once she runs a few tests, she finds the problem is more serious. The drivetrain connection is bad, causing the air conditioner to short. This will make her day a little longer than she'd hoped.

Daily Challenges

We like to think of cars as strong and sturdy. However, each car has its own quirks. Mechanics have to figure out the special needs of each automobile they work on. Car parts can also be extremely fragile. If car owners fail to maintain their vehicles, a messy layer of rust may coat their parts. Besides making a mechanic's job messier, the rust can also weaken car parts. Mechanics have to handle these parts with a light touch.

On the other hand, mechanics have to display some strength, too. They do a fair share of heavy lifting and spend a lot of time in awkward positions. They have to perform a lot of twists and turns to reach certain parts of cars. Of course, they also get very dirty from all the grease they work around.

Mechanics need to keep their focus on the task at hand. However, they also must think one step ahead. This will prevent dangerous accidents from happening. There are plenty of sharp objects in a garage that can cause cuts and bruises. Mechanics must also be careful not to get burned from torches and heated metal.

TAKING CARE OF BUSINESS

In 2000, about 840,000 men and women held jobs as automotive service technicians and mechanics.

CHAPTER FOUR

Popular Mechanics

Those mechanics who are passionate about their careers show a lot of dedication. They take pride in each car they repair.

The Next Level

Mechanics who show leadership can move quickly through the ranks. Within years, they can be promoted to shop manager. They may even supervise an entire staff.

Most mechanics work forty hours each week. Those who operate their own repair shops, however, will work longer hours. These mechanics must have a knack for business. They need to be able to hire a skilled staff to help them.

Today's repair garages can't function without mechanics who appreciate and understand the latest computer technology.

Tom and Ray Magliozzi must be the world's two most popular auto mechanics. They have millions of people following their advice. How do they find the time to deal with all those complaints? Well, the people who take their advice aren't customers—they're radio listeners.

The program *Car Talk* hit the airwaves of National Public Radio (NPR) in 1987. Listeners know the Magliozzi brothers by their nicknames, "Click and Clack." They chose these nicknames because they reminded them of sounds that old cars make. Tom and Ray used to run a do-it-yourself garage in a nearby town. In 1977, they began to discuss auto repairs and maintenance on the radio.

Each week, 2.3 million listeners tune in to their funny talk show. Listeners call in and describe the troubles they're having with their cars. Click and Clack then quickly diagnose the problem. They explain what needs to be fixed. They also guess what those repairs might cost.

Shop owners must also keep up good relationships with customers. Car owners need to be able to rely on their mechanics. If customers know they can trust their mechanics, they'll return to them for all their repairs.

Mechanics must carefully explain to clients what must be repaired. They must reassure them that they are trying to make the least expensive repairs possible. Suppose a car comes in with an engine that's not running properly. A mechanic would first check to see if the fuel filter was clogged. This would be a cheap repair. They would do this before pulling out and replacing the fuel pump, which would cost more money. If pulling the pump turned out to be an unnecessary repair, the customer would feel cheated out of hard-earned cash.

Car owners may not be able to skip work to bring their cars in for minor repairs. Because of this, many garages stay open late at night. Most are open for business on weekends. This allows customers to work around the demands of their own jobs. They can bring their cars in during their time off.

What Tomorrow Holds

As technology in the car industry changes, mechanics will have to continue to keep up. Newer cars have more body parts than older cars. These newer models are more difficult to work with. They require more expertise. Today's cars are often lighter than older cars. This means they are more likely to be damaged in an accident.

New vehicles are being built that run on alternatives to gas. Cars called Hybrid Electric Vehicles (HEVs) run on a mixture of gas and electricity. These amazing machines conserve fuel and help protect the environment. However, their electric systems operate on a high level of voltage. Mechanics must use caution when repairing HEVs. Some technicians have been electrocuted while servicing these high-voltage machines.

New cars such as this Honda Civic HEV help ease the burden on the environment. However, they also present mechanics with new challenges.

New technology will continue to improve the way cars run. However, the same technology will make the cars more complex. Because of this, auto repairers will be in greater demand. They will be expected to have formal training. They'll still need to work

well with their hands and have good problem-solving skills. Yet they will also need to know their way around complex computer systems. Those mechanics with a wide range of knowledge will be respected, relied upon, and well paid for their efforts.

apprentice (uh-**pren**-tiss) someone who learns a trade or craft by working with a skilled person

assembly line (uh-**sem**-blee **line**) an arrangement of machines and workers in a factory, where work passes from one person or machine to the next until it is complete

certification (suhr-te-fih-**ke**-shen) an act or document which proves someone has a certain level of expertise

coolant (**ku**-lent) an agent used to keep the temperature of a system below a certain level

corroded (kuh-**rode**-id) to be destroyed or eaten away little by little

diagnose (dye-ug-**nohss**) to determine the cause of a problem

expertise (ehk-sper-**tiz**) expert knowledge or skill

inspection (in-**spek**-shen) when a mechanic carefully looks over a car for any problems

manual (**man**-yoo-uhl) a book of instructions that tells you how to do something

repair order (ri-**pair or**-dur) notes and information about what was done to fix a car, and why

specialize (**spesh**-uh-lize) to focus on one area of work, or to learn a lot about one subject

technician (tek-**nish**-uhn) someone who works with specialized equipment

transmission (transs-**mish**-uhn) a series of gears that send power from the engine to the wheels

union (**yoon**-yuhn) an organized group of workers set up to help improve such things as working conditions, wages, and health benefits

vocational school (voh-**kay**-shuhn-ul **skool**) a school that provides special training for a job or profession

weld (**weld**) to join two pieces of metal or plastic by heating them until they are soft enough to be joined together

FOR FURTHER READING

Boraas, Tracey. *Auto Mechanics*. North Mankato, MN: Bridgestone Books, 1999.

Florian, Douglas. *An Auto Mechanic*. New York: William Morrow & Company, 1994.

Oxlade, Chris. *Car*. North Mankato, MN: Thameside Press, 2002.

Organizations

Automotive Youth Educations Systems
2701 Troy Center Drive, Suite 450
Troy, MI 48084
(248) 273-1200

**National Automotive Technicians
Education Foundation**
101 Blue Seal Drive, S.E. Suite 101
Leesburg, VA 20175
(703) 669-6650
www.NATEF.org

**National Institute for Automotive
Service Excellence**
101 Blue Seal Drive, S.E.
Suite 101
Leesburg, VA 20175
(703) 669-6600
www.asecert.org

Web Sites

U.S. Department of Labor
www.bls.gov/oco/ocos181.htm
This government Web site provides great information about the work done by auto mechanics. It mentions everything from working conditions to the future outlook for the job.

Click and Clack
www.npr.org/about/people/bios/magliozzi.html
This National Public Radio page features the bios for Tom and Ray Magliozzi (Click and Clack). The site also features audio clips of *Click and Clack* shows that you can download and listen to.

Car Talk
http://cartalk.cars.com/
The official Web site of America's most popular (and funny) mechanics, Tom and Ray Magliozzi. Plenty of information—from do-it-yourself tips to explanations of HEVs—can be found here.

INDEX

About the Author

Aileen Weintraub is a freelance author and editor living in the scenic Hudson Valley in upstate New York. She has published over thirty-five books for children and young adults.